Marriage Annulments *Under* POPE FRANCIS

Fr. William E. Young, Jr.

Imprimi Potest:
Richard Thibodeau, CSsR
Provincial, Denver Province
The Redemptorists

Imprimatur:
Most Reverend Timothy M. Dolan
Auxiliary Bishop, Archdiocese of St. Louis

Published by Liguori Publications
Liguori, Missouri
Liguori.org

ISBN 978-0-7648-2808-9

Originally published in 2002 by Liguori Publications
as *The What, Why, and How of Marriage Annulments*

Liguori Publications, a nonprofit corporation, is an apostolate of the Redemptorists. To learn more about the Redemptorists, visit Redemptorists.com.

Printed in the United States of America
18 19 20 21 22 / 5 4 3 2 1

Cover image: Catholic News Service

Foreword

While Pope Francis affirms the sacrament of marriage is a holy union that cannot be dissolved, he issued two apostolic letters in 2015, *Mitis Iudex Dominus Iesus* (The Lord Jesus, the Gentle Judge), and *Mitis et misericors Iesus* (Gentle and Merciful Jesus). In these letters, Pope Francis acknowledged there are circumstances in which a marriage can be annulled and announced a streamlined process for acquiring that annulment. This process went into effect December 8, 2015, at the launch of Pope Francis' Extraordinary Jubilee of Mercy.

Pope Francis signed the new law "for the purpose of implementing justice and mercy with regard to the truth of the bond to those who have experienced the failure of their marriage....The recently concluded Synod of Bishops expressed a strong exhortation that the Church draw near to 'the weakest of her members, who are experiencing a wounded or lost love' (*Final Report*, 55 [October 13, 2014]), to whom confidence and hope must be restored. Indeed, the laws now entering into force seek to show the Church's *closeness* to wounded families, with the desire that the many who experience the trauma of a broken marriage may be touched by the healing work of Christ, through ecclesiastical structures, in the hope that they discern that they are the new missionaries of God's mercy toward other brothers and sisters, for the benefit of the institution of the family."

—Pope Francis,
Rescriptum ex audientia,
December 7, 2015

Introduction

The Christian view of marriage is one where the couple enters into union with God and in God's grace fulfills and completes each other in their vocation of marriage. We see marriage and family as willed by God to help the spouses attain perfect happiness in eternal life with God. For these reasons, Christian marriage is both joyful and happy, as well as serious business.

Every gift God gives us has a divine purpose and intention. Our call is to live out—realize—that intention and purpose. The various teachings and regulations of the Church formulated through the centuries to govern marriage are intended to support the understanding of God's purpose and intention that marriage, when validly entered into, be unconditional, permanent (until death), and exclusive (wholehearted faithfulness between the spouses).

Marriage in the Bible

In the first book of the Bible, the Book of Genesis, we have two stories of creation (Chapters 1 & 2, respectively). God's decision to create humanity is very deliberate. Unlike the other creatures, humanity is created in God's own image and likeness. Humanity is also created gendered: male and female. The man and the woman recognize that each is made for—and given to—the other, and that out of all the creatures only another human being can complement, complete, and fulfill us:

> *Then the man said, "This at last is bone of my bones and flesh of my flesh; this one shall be called Woman, for out of Man this one was taken." Therefore a man leaves his father and his mother and clings to his wife, and they become one flesh.*
>
> GENESIS 2:23–24

The term "flesh" here is more than the physical body, or the physical union of sexual intercourse. "Flesh" here refers to the whole person, so marriage is intended by God to be a union of man and woman at every level and aspect of their persons (which is why any breach of trust invades the sacredness of the person and the holiness of the marriage bond). This is the "community of love" referred to in Church teaching. Sacred Scripture attests to the fact that God intends this union to be permanent and exclusive. Under the influence of God's revelation, the Jews gradually moved away from the prevalent surrounding culture of having multiple wives and concubines. What they held on to—and objected to letting go of when Christ revealed the fullness of God's plan for marriage—was divorce.

Where in the Bible can we find God's teaching on divorce?

In the Book of Malachi we hear God's final word on divorce in the Old Testament.

> *Because the LORD was a witness between you and the wife of your youth, to whom you have been faithless, though she is your companion and your wife by covenant. Did*

not one God make her? Both flesh and spirit are his. And what does the one God desire? Godly offspring. So look to yourselves, and do not let anyone be faithless to the wife of his youth. For I hate divorce, says the LORD*, the God of Israel, and covering one's garment with violence, says the* LORD *of hosts. So take heed to yourselves and do not be faithless.*

MALACHI 2:14–16

Jesus makes this teaching even more specific by adding a teaching on remarriage after divorce.

Some Pharisees came to him, and to test him they asked, "Is it lawful for a man to divorce his wife for any cause?" He answered, "Have you not read that the one who made them at the beginning 'made them male and female,' and said, 'For this reason a man shall leave his father and mother and be joined to his wife, and the two shall become one flesh'? So they are no longer two, but one flesh. Therefore what God has joined together, let no one separate." They said to him, "Why then did Moses command us to give a certificate of dismissal and to divorce her?" He said to them, "It was because you were so hard-hearted that Moses allowed you to divorce your wives, but from the beginning it was not so. And I say to you, whoever divorces his wife, except for unchastity, and marries another commits adultery."

MATTHEW 19:3–9

Saint Paul, likewise, teaches the sacredness of marriage and its permanent, binding nature.

To the married I give this command—not I but the Lord—that the wife should not separate from her husband (but if she does separate, let her remain unmarried or else be reconciled to her husband), and that the husband should not divorce his wife.

1 CORINTHIANS 7:10–11

The New Testament is full of teaching and examples concerning the love that spouses are intended to have for one another. Jesus used parables concerning marriage. Saint Paul wrote that a husband should love his wife as Christ loves the Church, laying down his very life for her (see Ephesians 5:25).

What, Why, and How

Divorce is so common in our society, why does the Church hang on to such old-fashioned teaching?

God's will and teaching are never out of date. It is the world that can fall out of step with God.

Where does the Church get the right to regulate marriage?

Believing that a marriage between a man and a woman is a sacred union, the Church is obliged to presume that every marriage, on the face of it, is valid and binding. Christ gave the apostles the responsibility of continuing his work of salvation, and this means that the Church has been given the authority to administer the sacraments and determine under what conditions they will be celebrated.

Why can't I just decide for myself that my marriage was invalid?

Celebration and administration of the sacraments belong rightly to the Church. The Church's whole orientation is to be as generous or liberal as possible with the conditions under which the sacraments can be celebrated. Sometimes, however, there are situations where something has occurred that needs to be cleared up before people in those circumstances can fully live the sacramental life. Divorce and remarriage are good examples. Christ entrusted the right and responsibility for this to people in leadership in the Church, not to every individual. There are many sacred actions or decisions that none of us can make for ourselves and which require that we submit to lawful, competent authority in the Church. For example, no one, not even a priest or bishop, can minister the sacrament of penance to himself. And a priest who wants to relinquish his ministry and marry cannot decide on his own to do that. He must submit his request to the authority of the pope.

Does the Church expect that I should have remained in a marriage where I was abused by my spouse?

Sometimes, despite the best intentions of one of the parties to the marriage, the other can make it impossible to stay in that marriage without jeopardizing the safety or spiritual welfare of the other spouse and/or children. In such a case, when all attempts at reconciliation have come to naught, the sad reality is that a civil divorce may be the only way to protect the rights of one of the spouses.

Civilly divorced after being married in the Church, am I free to date and enter a marriage by a judge or in another denomination?

No. This is a common misconception. The Church recognizes civil society's right to order marriage by just laws, and conforms its own marriage administration to just civil law, for example, the requirement to have a marriage license issued before the celebration of a marriage "in the Church." But a civil divorce does not affect the status of a couple who has been sacramentally married in the Church. While civil society doesn't care how many times you marry, get divorced, and remarry, as long as you do it in conformity with the civil law, the Church, faithful to the teaching of Christ, is unable to acknowledge divorce as well as remarriage without the benefit of an annulment. If you have married according to the laws of the Church—that's what getting married "in the Church" means, not in the church building—and get divorced, you are expected to conduct yourself as a married man or woman until you receive an affirmative decision from the Church as a result of an annulment procedure. To do otherwise is to choose to enter a situation "that objectively contravenes God's law" (*Catechism of the Catholic Church,* 1650).

Isn't the Church being cruel in not understanding my situation and seemingly preventing me from seeking happiness with a good and kind person after my traumatic divorce?

The Church and most priests sympathize deeply with the agonies and pains of every individual who has endured such trauma. Several things are worthy of consideration here. In the first place, following God's law will ultimately bring the most profound healing. Catholics have the great blessing of rich and clear teaching from the Church that we can be assured is the way to salvation for us. It is not always easy, but we can fully trust that God gives us greater gifts than we can imagine when we strive to remain faithful. Second, it is quite easy for an individual to make bad personal decisions right after coming out of a bad situation. Third, the truth is sometimes hard to hear and requires sacrifice and denial of self-will.

God and the Church want us to be happy. But the happiness God and the Church want for us goes beyond a happiness of "here and now"—it is eternal. Challenging teachings and regulations which support and define in practical terms how we ought to live are aimed at our eternal happiness and ultimate good. That's not cruelty. That's love. The annulment process is best seen as an indication of the Church's compassion in wanting to bring relief and liberation to people "stuck" in these difficult and often emotionally painful situations. To do so in a just and equitable fashion requires compliance with a reasonable procedure that will assist and preserve faithfulness of everyone involved to the dictates and will of the Lord.

Isn't an annulment just a "Catholic divorce"—replacing a civil divorce with its own form?

No. There is no such thing as "Catholic divorce," and it is misleading to call the annulment procedure "Catholic divorce." An annulment is a decision by highly trained people who make a judgment concerning a marriage. That decision answers the question whether what looked to be a "valid" or an "authentic" marriage actually was. These trained people look at the circumstances leading up to the marriage—the age, attitude, and understanding the parties to the marriage had about what they were doing—in order to determine whether the elements necessary to make a valid and authentic marriage were, in fact, present. If the decision is that they were not, the decision is "affirmative"; that is, the annulment is granted. If there are no grounds or evidence to indicate an invalid marriage, the decision is that the marriage is valid, and it stands. That's being faithful to God's commands concerning marriage.

What right does anyone have to pass judgment on me or my former spouse?

There is no personal character judgment involved in an annulment procedure. True, detailed information on the spouses, their family background, relationship, and marriage are required to be submitted to the tribunal—the officially established board which, in each diocese, deliberates and decides these matters—but no personal judgments are passed on anyone. The concern of the people who examine the various cases (called "judges") is only to determine whether the spouses at the time of marriage were knowledgeable enough about marriage, and capable of entering into a valid marriage with all the other essential elements being present. That's all. No character judgments are passed on anyone.

These judges—presumably all priests or unmarried people—what do they know about married life?

Wisdom and knowledge about marriage is not limited to the married. There *are* several priests on most of these tribunals, but there are also qualified married men and women, as well as single men and women. Regardless of vocation in life, these men and women are prepared by advanced studies, experience in life, and understanding of what are and are not healthy and valid conditions for marriage.

As part of Pope Francis' reform of canonical procedures, additional instruction is available in marriage and procedural law for canon lawyers, and additional preparation is available for marriage and family pastoral consultants.

Pope Francis reminds us that these generous people are providing "a service of souls, especially to those which are most wounded." They have great understanding of Church law, human nature, and life in general, or they wouldn't be serving in those positions.

Doesn't an annulment cost a lot of money?

There is a modest charge for the procedure because staff salaries have to be covered by the diocesan administration. No one, however, is denied the process because of the inability to pay. The fee can be reduced or completely waived if someone is unable to pay, or when paying it would be too burdensome.

How long does an annulment take?

It depends on the case load of the tribunal in your diocese, that is, how many people are applying for annulments. In addition, it depends on how quickly the person requesting (petitioning for) the annulment does his or her work on it.

Aren't annulments more quickly or easily granted if you are rich or of "importance" in the community?

No. In spite of the publicity garnered by some individual cases, all petitions for annulment are considered strictly on the merits of the information provided to the judges.

I have heard that the Church recently changed the annulment procedure, and that it takes much less time than in the past. Is that so?

In 2015 Pope Francis announced changes designed to streamline and simplify the annulment process for some cases. He said, "These measures have an eminently pastoral goal: to show the Church's concern for those faithful who are waiting for a quick verification on their marital status." Now annulments can follow one of two tracks. The ordinary process remains as described above in which a tribunal reviews the case, and then another tribunal from a different diocese must confirm any decision to grant an annulment.

In the newer, briefer process, the diocesan bishop, with the involvement of the pastor, can make a final decision to grant an annulment without involving a second tribunal. This saves time by placing the authority to make a final decision in the hands of the bishop and the tribunal where the petition was filed. However, the respondent must either actively participate in the brief process or agree to it without his or her active participation. Although the brief process may expedite matters, the underlying Church law about marriage and annulments remains the same. Your pastor or another knowledgeable person can explain further details and procedures, but keep in mind that the brief process requires the active participation of both parties. Failing that, the ordinary process must be followed.

If I am granted an annulment, will this make my children "illegitimate" since the Church is really saying that no valid marriage ever existed?

No. The judgment of the Church in granting an annulment has no effect on the legitimacy of children. If they were born within a marriage, even if that marriage is later declared null, there is no change in the status of children born in that union. Children carry no stigma at all if their parents' marriage ends in divorce—whether or not an annulment is granted. In any case, the term "legitimate" simply refers to the legal marital status of the parents, and whether a child was born within a legally recognized union. It says more about the legal status of the parents than the child. The Church never considers any child illegitimate.

Are some marriages annulled which shouldn't have been?

Perhaps. There has been some criticism of tribunals in the United States for the high number of annulments granted here. Critics interpret this number as an indication of a far too lax attitude toward the marriage bond. There are many reasons for this relatively high number, and the point could be debated. The judges make the best decisions they can based on the information provided to them. Is it possible that some people lie when submitting information? That is always a possibility, both here and in a variety of other circumstances. Information is provided to the tribunal under oath, so to lie would be committing the sin of perjury. Lying in order to get an annulment, however, defeats the whole purpose and intent of the petition, and whoever does so will eventually have to answer to God. Not only do they sin by lying, but they violate the sacred bond of the marriage which was falsely declared null, and commit adultery by entering into another union. Again, nothing is worth putting one's salvation in jeopardy.

Who can apply to the Church for an annulment?

Anyone who has experienced the tragedy of a failed marriage ending in divorce has a right to apply for the annulment, whether he or she plans on marrying again or not.